POEMS OF WAR

DUNCAN CULLMAN

authorHOUSE®

AuthorHouse™
1663 Liberty Drive
Bloomington, IN 47403
www.authorhouse.com
Phone: 833-262-8899

Published by AuthorHouse 03/07/2023

ISBN: 979-8-8230-0190-8 (sc)
ISBN: 979-8-8230-0192-2 (hc)
ISBN: 979-8-8230-0191-5 (e)

Library of Congress Control Number: 2023904102

Print information available on the last page.

Contents

Foreword

(TESTIMONY)

My steady girlfriend in 1974 was still Diane Stauder who was very good looking from Lorraine, Ohio. She found a job in Glenwood Springs at the world famous Hot Springs as a towel girl passing out towels and running the cash register at the thermally heated pool.

I had won the Nastar qualifying championships mayne a second behind Pepi Steigler of Austria, a former Olympic Gold Medalist and ahead of Spider Sabich who was less than a second behind me in third/ Bob Beattie of World Pro Skiing who also ran Nastar and the World Pro Ski Tour was doubly the sports agent for Spider Sabich. Beattie proclaimed a three way tie/ All three of us were to be awarded a "Zero" National Nastar Handicap.

Asked by Beattie what I had been doing for training I responded.

"Swimming laps in the Glenwood Pool"

"How did you accomplish that since it is not cheap"

"My girlfriend works there so I get to swim for free"

A few days later my girlfriend was fired / She said her boss told her he had to fire her because he got a phone call from Aspen from a business partner (Bob Beattie) to do so.

I, Duncan Cullman the Infernomeister, was such a threat to his darling Spider Sabich and the Palmer brothers from New Hampshire eventually also who signed with him so that behind the scenes he was actively ruining my life whenever possible from his Aspen desk.

"Your friends in Aspen got me fired" Diane told me. I didn't want to believe her. We argued. She said skiing was no good and by summer she left me. She went to Ireland with her girlfriend Jan but soon married a fisherman and had two sons. I never saw her again.

Turn Your Lives Around, Repent

You Russian tank Commanders turn your tanks around, repent / The enemy is not before you but behind you sending you to an early grave/The morning Star ★ is rising Venus / You cannot defeat Love 💕 it always prevails/Return to your families heroes when you mutiny against this evil/When you attack that monster in the Kremlin who tells lies/Who fabricates these hallucinations that your countrymen have been infiltrated by Nazis/Pravda the Truth is that you have been ordered to commit atrocities and war crime's/God is witnessing everything you do and you will be held accountable/What comes around goes around/This fire and destruction you sew you will reap also/Because Justice will prevail it always does in the end/The criminals will be caught and hung/Who led you to believe otherwise?/ You are loving a nightmare so go hang yourself to end it or attack Moscow/You see that is the only solution to your problem switch sides/Join with the Blue Morning ★ Ukraine and defeat Moscow forever ∞ because God in Heaven wills it so/ Bad Vlad shall hang and don't you join him on the gallows/Feel the rope around your neck tightening. with every war crime you commit/When you go home your families will disown you unless you kill Putin unless you'll kill Putin/Then you'll be the hero when you kill Putin or die trying to/ Then you're families will love 💕 you then sunflowers will be planted on your gravestones /You know deep in your hearts 💕 this is the awful truth Pravda that you want your own families to 💕 love you?

Everyone raised by the KGB had to believe all the lies and propaganda or else- The very sick Putin

Everyone raised in the former Soviet Union had to believe the state media or else

Thus it's deeply impaled in the Russian mind this loyalty to whatever the Czar believes must be true

The foreigners are all liars trying to take advantage of Mother Russia the big bear

So all her cubs are loyal to the point of death but why is Ukraine in disbelief

Perhaps those Greeks and their democracy penetrated her shores to trade with Vikings

So Mariupol is a Greek port then a Turkish port then a center of Jewish merchants and capitalists

God forbid those entrepreneurs on Soviet territory and dissidents like Navalny and Solzhenitsyn

So all the world is conspiring against Russia and She must fight back with Cyber Warfare

The deeply paranoid mother bear whose cubs included Iron Block nations

Now the senile Putin demands their return to Autocracy or else the current tantrum

Rockets, tanks and artillery for anyone who might doubt Putin's deep sincerity and love for Josef Stalin

So every Ukrainian city is now Stalingrad because deep in the dying mind of Putin

Nazis are once again invading the planet as well as the frontier of Russia so bring on the Cossacks

But Putin is the chief Nazi, Putin is the new Hitler, doubt him and be reduced to rubble, THE WORLD BEWARE!

Poetry In War

Vladimir P for Pogrom let it be known Athens and information have declared war

On you and your cronies for your sheer stupidity and ignorance how dumb can you be?

You have destroyed your own best ally in a tantrum of jealousy and then

You destroyed the lives of your best generals making them into war criminals killing children and the elderly

Your "Noble? War" is anything but noble and you are the epitome of a freak on drugs like Hitler

You must need some chemotherapy for your brain which is an aberration of hatred

For everything you cannot fathom including freedom and everything holy

Now that you are reprobate "living" in your self-created hell in the pale of death

What has Satan promised you and led you to believe that your Tomb would be unparalleled like Tutankamen in a Great Pyramid

Surely your jackals will be buried alive with you and your generals that have all failed you because you are mad and drove them mad as well

Now what shall be left of Russia after all of this has broken out like Covid a disease with no precedent other than Black Plague

Russia will be ruled by rats such as you and only fleas come to your assistance in your Mosque the Crimeland

You will wish you had never been born at least all your relatives think so already

You are an abomination like sin itself, you are selfishness gone berserk

Woe to you who hate

Woe to you who hate the Hebrew father of Jesus/Jesus was no Christian, It was Peter who started that organization. Aa for the trillionth gg of Jesus the Hebrew/ His mind is incomprehensible to us all/He is the Lord Almighty/Woe to you who hate out of ignorance because God is love/You have fallen from grace into blind selfishness like Putin/You desire to rule but everyone fears you/Love is what rules not fear.

Now War. So Fight

When Putin equals Hitler

How can it be any less than war

Ukraine defends itself against the Russian genocide

No different than Kosovo, no different than Serbia

China now wants to join in? Are they equally as crazy as Putin

To aid and abet war crimes and killing of unarmed citizens

Now it seems there will be chemical and biological war as well

Of course this must include a new Covid variant

These are certainly the end times, didn't Notrodamus envision

A shoulder fired weapon like the Stinger and pestilence

All of this part of the great overdue reduction of human population

The planet it seems cannot stand so many of us contributing to global warming

All the Mammals are now in peril and we ourselves an endangered species

Because Putin is a madman and these Autocracies believe their own propaganda and lies

So God punished Israel with draught and famine for not going to war

For not waging war on the heathen Yahweh was angry

So now what is God thinking for it will surely come to pass

The strong arm of righteousness will deliver a blow in the name of Truth and Justice

God is patient and kind, slow to anger and quick to forgive

Evil demands punishment and death and krishna sounds his Conches

It is the noise of righteous war, it is the sweet sound of the Victory of the Good

Please join the fight for the oppressed against the oppressor who is under the spell of the evil one

Please enlist your service in whatever you can do to deliver the army of God

Which is morality and Truth is its breastplate like yours as we were born to be soldiers on the winning side

God is in control not Putin, if we must die then let it be for Good

Jesus is waiting for us in Heaven, Jesus is waiting for us to choose him not our portfolios

There is a war going on and we must choose sides, the right one

Or God will be angry with us, or God will be very angry with us

The other side has taken the field and the sports contest is to begin

Aren't we going up to bat? Aren't we stepping out there or are we just cowards

Then we deserve to die. Then we deserve to die anyway, so fight!

The Very Good News I am Solzhenitsyn's Protégé

The very good news is that I am Solzhenitsyn's protege. You see, I wrote to him in 1985 from Telluride, Colorado and told him in my best Russian that I enjoyed his book. He replied after a month from his home in Cavendish, Vermont that my Russian wasn't very good and that apparently I didn't understand his book at all. In fact, he called me an "Idiot" but I took it as a compliment because I had when quite young read Dostoevsky's book 'The Idiot".

That was all thirty-seven years ago and I have had time to mull over his book "August 1917" which I do admit I did not fully understand completely at first reading. So I have thought about it for thirty-seven long years and that is why I am Solzhenitsyn's protege. I am older and just slightly wiser now and I read Gulag Archipelago by Solzhenitsyn as well though years ago.

Absolute power corrupts absolutely. Didn't someone say that? Stalin, Mao, Hitler and Putin are all among the very worst despots of modern times. Jesus could have chosen to lead an insurrection but chose not to because it would have led to evil and suffering. He suffered alone instead.

The very good news is that I am Solzhenitsyn's protege....

I must make a choice but you don't feel compelled

I must make a choice, hot or cold? Because if I am like warm I might die as a bystander signifying nothing You can do as you please that is freedom. While I have decided that God is good so Jesus leads me. You can decide differently. So I am siding with Ukraine while you might be indifferent or choose Russian oil or Putin. So be it. I have to live with my conscience while you may not have one? I used to think you were hot but lately your friends are now just like warm Maybe I never knew you at all and that's why we didn't marry. Good thing then that we go separate ways You boarded that flight to Moscow. That would not be My choice. Anyway take care of yourself and all that ambition of yours to see Red Squirrel. I hear the wind is changing direction please be careful. Goodbye

Supporting All Ukrainians

So very easy it is for us to support Ukrainians in their defense of their homeland

They remind us of farmers in Michigan or Wisconsin or even Minnesota or Indiana

When they become older they fill giant section 8 apartment complexes like Chicago or Detroit

They have broken their backs working all their lives like Americans to earn some retirement

Here comes the Russian Army across their border to steal away everything and

Send everyone running to their basements like scared animals from explosions and bullets

Black smoke fills the sky and everywhere there are fires and debris clogging the streets

Some retirement this is as the world's richest man, Putin, attacks them with flamethrowers and bombs

While I sit in my comfortable living room with water, heat and lights

It is still snowing everywhere, in both America and Ukraine

What is this madness unfolding? Our own climates are severe enough

This Putin is obsessed with hatred, torture and killing and his people mostly applaud him

That damned Kremlin and those damned large other buildings in Moscow are out to conquer

All the Metro Stations underground full of silent camper refugees

The bombardment up above them, rockets raining down and artillery shells exploding

I can hear all this noise from my television set in America and South America, Asia and Oceania

After seventy seven years Europe is in the midst of war again! Russian tanks roll through suburbia

"Nato has given Putin the green light to go on safari, mass graves in ditches everywhere

Teens, children and the elderly all dead lined up in ditches, shot and tortured

Russian people have given Putin the green light to conquer their neighbors

The scale and magnitude of these atrocities is overwhelming, crows and buzzards eat the bodies

Nobody outside of Russia is cheering for this mad Russian army, we are horrified

I will go to my local Army & Navy Store and buy a helmet and canteen

So I can feel appropriate in front of the war correspondents CNN

Everyone is cheering for Ukraine! Everyone is praying for Ukraine!

Everyone but a Russian is supporting Ukraine!

The Day of the Lord

So help us God because babies, mothers and grandmothers

Are starving and homeless, freezing and bleeding so that I personally

As a citizen of Earth must uphold my responsibility and duty

To declare war against all this unnecessary evil and its perpetrators

Who have broken every law every written, not just one

Thus they are committed to hell bound destruction by their immorality

They beg for death to ease their guilt and suffering so will I slay them

I shall destroy them with the sword that is Truth I will vindicate the people of God

Righteousness shall be my breastplate and armour and I shall no longer fear

Because I am innocent in the eyes of God my Redeemer

He shall raise me up at death unto the new life eternal to be with Him in paradise

So let me sleepwalk among my enemy who are drunk from so much killing

I will kill them as they sleep and I will kill them when they wake up

I will hunt them down and pursue them in every corner of this Earth

Wherever they go they shall not escape the wrath of the Lord Who is in hot pursuit

My land shall know peace again because I shall have trampled them underfoot

All their blood and bones are nothing more than fertilizer

It is now the Day of the Lord, now and forevermore, Hallelujah!

You Muscovites Be Aware

You Muscovites be aware your fate will be identical to Mariupol

However that siege ends in Mariupol the very same ending will befall you

Whether it will be in fifty days or fifty years no one can be certain

What you have sewed will be reaped upon you says the Lord Most High

Well you don't believe in God anymore now that you have your Putin-Kahn

You don't believe in these fairy tales about your cyber warfare against the entire planet?

Be afraid anyway! Be afraid for the Day of the Lord which is coming soon

Be afraid for Mariupol that is starving to death that will be your fate also soon

You cocky Russian soldiers with all your artillery shells and rockets the day is coming

The very long night of your worst fear is arriving and you will run out of shells and bullets

The Babushkas will charge you with pitchforks and sabers your end is not so very distant

Tell your commanders to turn their armies around to face the real enemy V. Putin-Kahn who has betrayed you all

His personal greed is destroying Russia and what will be left when China captures Siberia?

Dear Vladimir

Great leader Vladimir Putin/ How we love and forgive you as uneasy as this may seem/ You need to search your own heart /Didn't your mother love you when she changed your diaper?/Or were you raised by wolves?/Surely someone loved you/ Reflect and remember/ You have been going through some lonely and paranoid times/It is not healthy to live so far from your family and friends/The whole world is scared as you fire hypersonic missiles costing a hundred million dollars each/Love does not cost money and really is a better bargain/ Aren't you a smart shopper?/Stop this nonsense called war/ It is scaring everyone yet uniting them in their love for one another/ While you are not so loved unless of course you choose peace and to be a peacemaker

The Gang in the Kremlin

With the collapse of Communism in Russia those who ran the back
markets

Were the only organized understructure essentially the mob of
criminal smugglers

Therefore it was the mafia itself plus elements of former KGB like
Putin

Who became the new government and being the underworld itself
they stifled all criticism

So Russia and Putin are ruled by the devil and everything dark and
sinister

Therefore do not expect any quick solution to this catastrophe in
Ukraine

Putin is shoring up support by convincing Russians that the whole
world is ganging up on them

Rather it is the Kremlin gang itself that is threatening the entire world
with its criminality

Sacerdote in the Kremlin

Sacerdote is now in the Kremlin from which emits fire, lightening and shrapnel

The thirsty Politboro is ding on Ukraine citizens and fires cruise missiles at section 8 housing

Wherever there is a high concentration of population the Mongol Khan Putin aims his artillery and bombs

The highest priority military targets in Ukraine are chickens, housepets and babies all of whom collect Ukrainian Easter eggs

Sacerdote Putin seems to be targeting the aging Babushkas who remind him of his mother?

When will the bloodletting cease when will Putindote withdraw his vampire straw?

From the 38th great
ggggggggggggggggggggg
grandson of Vladimir of Kiev

Other Vladimir from Ulan Bator and Moscow

I am not happy with you for killing so many of my distant cousins and terrifying my Babushkas

A thousand years has passed and I am alive in my descendants who are united in defense

Swedes and Greeks traded along these my fat swollen rivers, they intermarried

Thousands of years passed and thousands of great harvests with nobody starving

Until Stalin and Hitler and you Putin decided on campaigns of terror and evil

From your deep basement beneath the Kremlin and your innumerable Dachas

How can a person of so much immeasurable wealth detest and hate those less fortunate?

Have you gone mad? What was her name, or is it your own mother you hate?

Did your favorite horse die or your many favorite dogs begin to growl at you?

Who can approach you the devil incarnate, the master of deceit and lies

So your best advisors it is speculated would rather lie to you because the truth is foreign

The Truth Pravda is now a fleeting foreigner who has run away to Tallinn

The Truth has left this whole generation of Russians for the sake of the KGB

Paranoia now lives in Moscow like in times of Stalin anyone can be arrested

Just for sneezing which might be translated into criticism of the Beast who now rules

The Beast with the long tail has risen into all the suburbs of Moscow and her puppets

Liars are rewarded and distortion is the status quo while soldiers die for their war crimes ordered by you

Yes these dark days of evil will have an end and the vile and disgusting will burn in this holy fire destroyed armored carriers

All this blood soaking the ground it cries "Avenge Me" it is the blood of Christ All shed for you because you are evil and absurd driven by madness which has overcome you\

Russia you once had friends and allies but who can trust you when you turn against your closest neighbors?

You will die alone and forgotten and your history will be burned with you a great fire against a late autumn darkening sky

And there will be no Christmas in Moscow while in Kiev I shall ride on my white horse through the streets of cheering children and grandparents

Ukraine the Victory is ours and the Truth will not be denied nor the love!

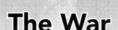

The War

Now that peace is shattered by Russian bombs, tanks and missiles

It's war.

A war by the Mongol Hordes against civilized Europe in the Ukraine

Where the Greek Empire traded with Vikings on the immense rivers

Creating a bountiful harvest of wheat and Sunflowers, prosperity and population

Large apartment complexes to heat more cheaply in winter and create some shade in summer for breezes

That Mongol Khan in his Mosque he does not care much for people

He wants to shed their blood for fertilizer and make what's left into chili

He sends out his army like Montezuma to capture children for sacrifice

He commands his subjects and generals like Sacerdote who wears a golden helmet

Meanwhile NATO responds like a herd of bleating sheep, okay let the monster eat just those Ukrainian sheep and be satisfied

Sacerdote and Montezuma and Ghenghis Khan all whet their appetites for more blood on the horizon

The "Butcher of Syria" General Ivanovich he is no different with his metal straw he pokes to suck even more blood not less

All the stock markets hope for an early ending to this war so that gas prices will drop

Promised weapon systems to Ukraine arrive late while Mariupol starves to death after ten thousand artillery rounds flatten every building

Thousands are dying and thousands of more will soon die in Ukraine while Russia suffers only devaluation of the Ruble

Where is Justice, where is God? Where is the army of Liberation amassed by the Allies who are on the side of good for goodness sake?

Putin, You Are No Hero

Putin, you are no hero

You only destroy lives you do not save any including your own

You did all this to shore up your reputation as great leader

Whoever follows you is a war criminal and co-conspirator in murder

Of course that's how you made all your money, killing everyone in your path

Of course we respect you out of fear because torture is your game and assassination

So a peace treaty is meaningless with you and a cease fire just prolongs our negligence

In Russia you are "Man of the year" every year like the Tsar was

While in the rest of the world, you are considered to be the "Number one enemy of peace and a menace"

Your navy bullies the oceans and your planes overhead, well there are less of them now

Your pilots and you imagine they will be buried beneath the Kremlin wall

All to some great tune played by a Soviet Orchestra

You are both despised and hated more than you realize

Anyone who would love you faces an early grave so you are

Not my hero, no. Putin, you are no hero at all. Throw all your medals in the garbage

Dear Vladimir II,

You have one last chance: you must admit you made a mistake and now that you have found "Krishna" you have decided for peace and will attend "Rave Concerts" like "Woodstock", ride naked on your horse again and stay longer on the mountains during" Ski Vacations".

Otherwise we cannot help you any further. You will run out of hypersonic missiles at ten billion roubles each. You will run out of MIG 35s. Your enemies believe in Jesus that He will rescue them on the "Final Day" no matter if you nuke them or not. They have decided not to be afraid of you.

So crawl out of your Kremlin Bunker into the light of day and apologize to your people; that you led them into such a big economic and military mess. Pull your troops out of Ukraine and tell them to go home to their wives and take a hot bath. Believe me that they need to.

Summon your assistants and give them cyanide pills if they decline "Hippy" drugs and ski vacations. You would all be better off on a train to Siberia and the Gulag where the Chinese army happily awaits your arrival.

One last request is that from your now embezzled fortunes you build new apartment houses in the Ukraine for the over six million and growing homeless displaced Ukrainians, they can't all go to Israel or Poland. There simply isn't room enough even in Antarctica.

Some of your closest fans should take the hint and go to "Woodstock" with you maybe on horseback if enough horses are still alive.

All my sincere apologies that this didn't work out quite as you planned it and I am not saving a room for you in Heaven unless you change your ways,

God

The Resurrection of My Ukraine

To assist you in your defense of our Homeland I Vladimir 1 of Kiev have directed my many great great grandchildren from many parts of this Earth to join in defense to repel the invader sent by Satan to destroy us but our numbers now are like sands of the sea we are infinite like swirling snowflakes so Mr. Putin recall your army to Moscow shy do did you fight your own countryman, are you playing Russian Roulette inside the Kremlin what about the book of life? Or have you left the land of the living such as Ukraine to live in a land of death Russia this will be the end of you and bang the gun goes off and the bullet enters your own skull alas you will be forgotten and your name erased from the book of Life....

Scared and Lonely On the Russian Front

If I were a brainwashed Russian would I follow Putin off the cliff into the sea?

If I had been born in Germany would I have joined the "Brown Shirts?"

I would hope that my parents loved me enough to explain the consequences of evil

Left to my own designs would I have joined a gang of bullies?

Drafted into the Russian Army and told we were liberating Ukraine

Would I even sense that killing women and children is a justifiable act of war?

In a land of no freedom how would I even imagine what freedom is?

So if my leader orders me to fight a "Noble War" of Russian Imperialism

Who am I to disagree and be demoted and be sent to a concentration camp in Siberia for re-education?

My Russian leader is a devil with horns and I am Satan's disciple the Russian soldier

Doesn't the rest of the world envy Russian military might? Or are they as scared and lonely as I am now in hell?

Information and knowledge will defeat ignorance and distortion

In this war information and knowledge will defeat ignorance and distortion

It is the battle for truth and justice which always win

Even though material wealth may be compromised

Money and Putin's money don't necessarily determine the outcome

Though money buys missiles, tanks and planes these weapons

Don't themselves produce dividends and more often just craters

So there is no guaranteed bonus for Putins' investment in arms

Just sweat, blood and tears of his own people whom he sacrifices like pawns in a game of chess

He is a monster with no feelings, a Sacerdote Ptin Khan Great Mongol

There is a quantitative end to his efforts once every rocket has been fired

All of this misery will backfire because Russian mothers will cry over missing sons

Who will help these mothers and when they grow old surely not the dead

What does Putin care for he is death personified, the devil incarnate

The world's richest man Putin on a fast track to his own self destruction

And the suicide of the Russian Empire, why?

Vladimir let me apologize

Vladimir let me apologize for everything I have said

If you decide for peace and a ceasefire to all this chaos

Then we who claim to be Christians will have to forgive you

But if not then let us piss on your grave because many a Babushka

Wants to strangle you with her bare hands so let them all have access to you

All of them without heat and food with no hot water and no bed to sleep upon

Far over a million are they whose lives you have compromised or killed

I cannot guarantee they will ever forgive you because your crimes are so horrific

So let them all piss on you instead let them piss on the Kremlin as well

As for that other large building of the Soviets near Red Square

Let it be museum of Russian atrocities to display the great shame of the Russian people

As for Red Square let it be painted a different color and forgotten

And as for your descendants let them be ashamed forever because you are an embarrassment to every generation

Bucha Atrocities, War Crimes, Torture

In Bucha, there were no dead Ukrainian soldiers as the citizens exited for heaven and eternal life/As for the dozens of burning tanks well someone must have thrown 200 Molotov Cocktails/ So there were no civilian casualties S everybody hates Putin and his harem/ There are no civilians left in Ukraine and everyone is now a soldier/ Babushkas attack with pitchforks, dogs growl and babies cry for freedom/ Ukraine will live!

Blue Morning Star Ukraine, Sunflower Rising (Bucha 2)

No one here has died in vain

No one in Bucha has died in vain

The ocean of the dead

In the vast Wheatfield Ukraine

Will again be filled with Sunflowers

As soft summer, breezes shall massage us in warm sunshine

Children will once again play on swingsets

Children will play with toy soldiers

Then they grew up to become an army

To defend the Blue Morning Star Ukraine

Against the red planet of Putin

These Soviet tanks will be flowerpots

In memory of the brave civilians armed only with Molotov cocktails

Riding out on bicycles or running on foot to halt the world's largest tank battalion

And stop it here in Bucha and inflame it's tank treads

For the defense of all things holy, children dogs and chickens

The Ukraine will rise and live

And "Mother" Russia will be no more, she became a harlot under Putin

He sold out his own mother, there is no more love in Russia

While Ukraine is all the love while Ukraine is basking in the soft sunshine of victory everlasting and eternal

Written into the Book of Life Bucha where citizens have risen among the Angels

Cherubs defended Bucha to defeat the devil himself Vlad the Bad

Only what is good will prevail everything bad will fade away

Ukraine so good always and forever the Sunflower rising

Russia Is Sociopathic

Russia has been on a very bad parh for quite some time and is now still very much a sociopath. There is no getting close to a sociopath without being taken advantage of. A sociopath can never be considered a friend, maybe a dangerous acquaintance. But who needs one?

Russia borders many nations but who can trust her? Absolutely no one can trust her as she is just a game player who only plays if she can better herself at the expense of others. It wasn't always this way as Peter the Great was hardworking and humble. That was three hundred years ago and times have changed.

This must be terrible news to all Russian citizens. Many have packed their bags and left for permanent vacation. If I were a Russian I would rent a sailboat. The ocean is probably friendlier than Vladimir Putin. Vladimir Putin is a psychopath. Russia has chosen to follow a sociopath.

There will be consequences, where will you run to?

There will be consequences to this new morality you inspire among your subjects Putin Khan

Because for centuries the original morality established by God and Moses, Krishna, Buddha and Mohammed

Declared cleanliness to be closest to godliness not this mess you bring on others with artillery tanks bombs and missiles

Of course you are your own god, rich and narcissistic self-serving

As for the Russian people in their secure cities all that they are missing are a few food stuffs plus their sons and a daughter or two

They went off to a military exercise which turned into a World War and you set them up to be hanged as war criminals like you and your generals

Some great friend and leader you turned out to be the devil incarnate

So now you threaten chemical and nuclear war in your tantrum against the democracies

I think the West has had enough of you by now every night on television you reign down destruction and death

You yourself are immune to these cruise missiles in your Dacha you eat caviar and sip Chardonnay

The Germans might send ten thousand nuclear soldiers to Latvia and the French ten more thousand to Hungary then the Italians ten thousand to Romania and the Spanish then the Swedes and Greeks and the Dutch while the Americans and Brazilians to Sakhalin

Yes there will be consequences and soon Justice will reign down like a river, the mighty Volga, Don and Mississippi and the Amazon, Tigris and Euphrates

Where will you hide when they come for you? Where will you run to?

Good Friday 2022

Now that Jesus has been crucified on Golgotha Hill which is like a town dump

Putin wants to crucify Ukraine as well for its defiance and disbelief of Soviet Ideology

Mostly a fabrication of lies to justify continuing lies to justify this war of destruction

In which fifty million lives are already at stake this is truly a war

Between the Greek Empire and democracy including Rome and Western Civilization

And the Barbarian horde of Putin Khan, Chief Mongol so the nations line up in defense

It is not just Ukraine that is at war, it is civilization itself trying to breath clean air

This Crucifixion and bloodletting is so dirty that the sky turns terribly black at noon

Apparently evil has been unmasked and personified by Vladimir Putin

Who threatens Finland, Sweden and the West with hypersonic rockets, bombers and armored vehicles

The rock is rolled in front of Jesus 'tomb and Herod is defiant so is Putin screaming

"There will be consequences" to anyone doubting Putin, world dictator

While we know deep in our hearts that Jesus will be seen resurrected on the shores of Lake Galilee

So will Ukraine too rise from ashes and death and Spartan troops will raise their banners

Because it is Easter and what is good and best will persevere this darkness and tragedy for all of the Russias

Putin Continues to Threaten the Planet with His Tantrum and Where is God?

Putin continues to threaten the planet with his tantrum and bad sandbox toys

Missiles and ships, bombs and artillery plus tanks and nasty Russian generals

While Nato shudders and hides because of its thirst for Russian oil

Germany and Austria plus Hungary declare dependence on Russian natural gas and this has allowed the Ruble to recover

Apparently his stomach bothers him so he is attacking Russia's underbelly Ukraine

How can one despot cause so much pain and suffering?

The world must be overpopulated we know that so Putin is now calling for total war

It seems almost imperative to the free world to destroy this Putin fleet barricading the Black Sea and Sea of Azov

Then the Ukrainian coast can be liberated and resupplied to resist this Putin Mongol Horde

The Mongols had respect at least for animals but Putin is much more like Hitler

He has made Hitler look like a babe in swaddling clothes with toy rattles

The West and Nato should show some resolve and send a missile from

Antarctica and level the Kremlin as well as the Cyber HQ

Everyone will cheer including the angels in heaven to see retaliation and Justice

Where is God with His Hammer and a scythe to take revenge for all this human and animal suffering?

Where is God?

Western Countries Should Leap Into the Defenses of Mariupol and Kharkiv

The Western Democracies should leap into the defense of democracy in Ukraine and stop making excuses or living in denial. WWIII is here and now there is no avoiding it. Putting off a response in total to Putin will only make it worse down the road. Putin plans to annex the Baltic States after Moldava and the Russian war machine will grow with captured new territories enslaving and holding hostage everyone in their Draculan path.

Countries like Brazil but not necessarily Brazil with huge unemployment should mobilize their national guards and send their officers and elite units into the fight in Ukraine or else wait a few months and face China and Korea as well.

There is no escaping the fact that Putinflation will trigger world recession which can only be countered by war economies which will at least guarantee full employment and stimulate the floundering economies of the third world.

Russian rockets are not unlimited in supply and their factories which produce them and ships which fire them must be bombed and torpedoed.

There is little or no time to waste on these rogue imperialistic dictatorships which will soon all awaken to Western apathy and cowardly inaction.

We should practice weekend evacuation of our large cities for possible extended vacations in bomb shelters as a preclusion to looming expanded world war.

No doubt about it now that Putin and his cronies are planning world genocide of everyone in their way. The time is here to fight not to cower.

Putin claims moral victory but the Victory is Putin's Madness

Putin who is devoid of any morals claims perhaps a "Morale" victory

After destroying and burying Mariupol population over 400.000 now just a few hundred

Unknowingly Putin has awaken the sleeping giant of Greek Democracy whose empire he imagined dead

Now it has reawakened from its sleep and Sparta's long forgotten soldiers have descendents recently born to reclaim Greece

Soon Greek submarines will be on patrol sinking Russian ships in the Bosporus and beyond

Poseidon is rising and Atlantis with it while Peter the Great is deeply ashamed

How can one man Putin embarrass all of Russia with his dementia

The only victory in Russia is the victory of madness in Putin at the expense of every Russian citizen

The Difference Between Us Is A Chasm Wide-Defeat For Russia

The difference between us Vlad is a very wide chasm

You may win many opening battles and even kill most of us

But we are Christians and not criminals like you and there is a wide chasm

Separating us from temptation and hell into which you have fallen unknowingly

So we can cross ourselves and go into battle full well knowing we live and die for goodness sake

While your lives have no meaning other than rape, lust and killing

You hide all that with a military uniform you imagine but God knows

God knows you are wicked beguiling liars of no conscience on a direct path to hell

Rockets, smoke and bullets all attest to your pathway into great destruction

The innocent dead are already in heaven with God where you will be barred from entrance because the light is too bright

The bright light of truth surrounding God will unmask you so go hide

Go hide in deepest darkest night with all your lies and false propaganda

How many more seconds will you be allowed in this world of life when you espouse death and destruction

While my time here on Earth is passing like sand through the hourglass in awe of the majesty of Truth

You are showing signs of illness and sickness even mental retardation and decline

Vlad being evil had some short term successes but in the long run you will be alone and abandoned in utter defeat

Pharoah and his army

Listen you Egyptians in your chariots and tanks

You are nothing more than slaves who have been whipped into battle unwillingly

Because you are killing grandmothers and grandchildren whom you are told is the enemy

Actually they are your cousins so the blood you are spilling is your own

Though this madness cannot continue indefinitely because there will be a reckoning by God

Who will intervene in your crimes and end your life painfully

No chance to see your families and say goodbye but they will have disowned you

Because Putin is your god whom you adore but realize he only loves himself not you

You have been abandoned by love into the hell of unpopular war

Following orders but if you have a cruise missile point it at the Kremlin and wake up those inside

Jolt them back into Justice Arriving On Earth sent by God so much for slavery

Join a revolution inside yourself be for truth and justice and freedom

Russia may survive without Putin but with Putin is on a path of self-destruction

You can feel the wind blowing and there will be a new season after this war

Where will you be when it's over six feet underneath or with the Angels instead?

Putin Wishes To Annex Moldova And New York

Vlad the Bad seeks to liberate Russian citizens and Mongols trapped behind lines in the free world. Rumania, Hungary, Poland, Lithuania, Germany and France are all on his agenda as his thirst for blood is unquenchable. The Sacerdote of the Kremlin wants you and your children for a special "Chili" dinner in the Kremlin to be served with Tartar Sauces from previous conquests

Midnight Again

It's midnight again here and soon will be or was everywhere else

Though we don't understand fully why God takes away everything we have just to give it back

So perhaps these short mortal lives of ours he will surely take them all away

In order to grant us new bodies and eternal lives as Angels singing hymns for you

So tonight we are asking you about Ukraine and how everyone there has lost a great deal

Mostly they are still alive and struggling against everything Russia and Putin hurl their way

Missiles, bombs, artillery shells and tanks plus snipers: not a very good day there nor night

Putin assassinates or jails all opposition and rules entirely by fear like Stalin

So he is like the very worst gangster on the planet plus he has the nuclear button

The Western democracies are all in denial of WWIII because it will mean great destruction

Of both property and lives, we could very easily be bombed back into the Stone Age or worse

So anyway supposing the West gets back their courage and launches a pre-emptive attack of non-nuclear cruise missiles against Russia

But we all know that won't happen because the stock markets will tumble and there ...

There will be no dividends and no bonuses at Christmas when everyone expects lots of presents under the Tree

So we have to watch all these horrors on television 24/7 of Russian State terrorism

So in Russia everyone works for the Mafia more or less, it is a Criminal State

Therefore the Russian people are responsible for Putin they shore him up in abeyance

It is now impossible for Russians to believe that Putin is moral and or claims "Moral Victory" in Ukraine

There is nothing moral about killing civilians and shelling apartment complexes

One in every eight Ukrainians has fled to Poland or another European neighbor

Mostly the ones who fled had either cars, money or both and many just had feet and the clothes on their backs

Europe needs Russian gas and oil and is unlikely to bomb their oil supply directly

Russia feels it must flex its muscle, test its army and weapons, navy and cruise missiles

So Navalny returns to Russia and is arrested as are all the dissidents

Ghengis Putin Khan Sacerdote with his straw for human blood he sucks like Count Dracula

We know what the final result of evil will be, we know Al Cappone went to Alcatraz

Stalin died in his sleep unlike Mussolini and Hitler so how will it be looking under the Christmas Tree this year with these high gas prices?

Battleground Ukraine is becoming a wasteland unfit for human habitation just an ongoing Russian Revolution

Russia Is A Pariah And An Uncivilized War Criminal

Because Russia Is A pariah and uncivilized war criminal it should be BANNED FROM the United Nations. It has a right to veto any resolution passed by the United Nations? Why?

The United Nations must raise its own armies from its member states and send them into Ukraine. Perhaps two hundred thousand professional soldiers from two hundred nations.

Russians and North Koreans who threaten the world with nuclear war should be hung for terrorism.

World War II is here and now and may end up being fought with sticks and stones but fight we must not cower to these bullies!

Following Putin Off A Cliff

If I were a brainwashed Russian would I follow Putin off the cliff into the sea?

If I had been born in Germany would I have joined the "Brown Shirts?"

I would hope that my parents loved me enough to explain the consequences of evil

Left to my own designs would I have joined a gang of bullies?

Drafted into the Russian Army and told we were liberating Ukraine

Would I even sense that killing women and children is a justifiable act of war?

In a land of no freedom how would I even imagine what freedom is?

So if my leader orders me to fight a "Noble War" of Russian Imperialism

Who am I to disagree and be demoted and be sent to a concentration camp in Siberia for re-education?

My Russian leader is a devil with horns and I am Satan's disciple the Russian soldier

Doesn't the rest of the world envy the Russian military? Or are they scared?

Mariupol And The Causeway To Freedom

Mariupol on the causeway to freedom

Whose valiant defenders under poles of smoking steel

Bombarded by the Vandals who have sacked Rome and would so again

The Sacerdote monster Putin from his Castle Transylvania the Kremlin

His armies marching the globe in genocide in support of Autocracy everywhere

To enslave humankind with his robot Zombie army and battleship Mosqeva

While in San Antonio at the Alamo two hundred fifty resist Santa Ana with five thousand

George Washington on his white horse declined to be a king he freed some slaves

Though father Abraham freed them all and paid with his life

There are idiots who prefer a dictator who does all their thinking for them

Putin's Army of Idiots firing their guns and in wrong direction

Now let us consider our own future shall we not come to the aid of Mariupol

In a dignified war of righteousness to restore freedom and liberate the captives

Let freedom ring and let the Kremlin burn for its crimes against humanity

Because of the vanity of one sick mind and his Oligarchs we have this war

Let the Bells of Freedom ring over the land in Kiev and Philadelphia and Paris

Let tyrants beware that men are more intelligent and not monkeys in trees anymore

We will resist against your convenient lies and racial bigotry

We will resist under piles of steel in bomb shelters and train stations everywhere

Because I hear the Freedom Bells ringing everywhere so I will join the fight

To destroy the oppressor and liberate the captives everywhere and

We are not alone anymore we are gathering an army of liberation a band of brothers of every color and every creede

Do To Moscow Exactly What Has Been Done To Mariupol

It's only fitting and just to do unto Moscow what it has done to others. There will be no end to this war until Moscow its perpetrator is eliminated and a smoking ruin. Everything Moscow stands for is evil: her lies and deceit, her cyber war and war crimes. She is a pariah, a Jezebel.

As for Putin who climbed onto that throne of darkness, the Kremlin, he deserves the same fate, to be exiled to Siberia and fittingly be enslaved before he takes his cyanide pill which must be close to his bedside.

As for the Russian people who are not in Moscow they are more distant and possibly innocent to some measure, but Moscow is well aware of her mission and purpose to serve hell and its demons. So proximity to Putin is the key, whoever loves that devil will ultimately hate himself.

Woe to Moscow you are a city of doom and despair and unlike Berlin which was rebuilt after WWII you will be just a dusty wasteland, a dump for all your broken armored vehicles, missile fragments, chemical and biological warfare stockpiles, a garbage pit nothing more.

Defend Civilization Against Barbarism

Defend civilization against barbarism

Defend human rights against those who would remove them

Defend charity and compassion against greed and avarice

Defend children from harm

Defend us Lord against our adversaries though we walk through a valley of darkness

Protect us with the inner light of your wisdom and love

Against the evildoers who espouse ignorance to bring clouds without rain

Defend us when large superpowers fire missiles and drop bombs on us

Because we are believers in your divine mercy and compassion for life

You lead us as though with a lamp on a straight road to victory and truth

There is no night there in the presence of the Lord we are convinced

He shall come for us on our final day in our final minute he will raise us up

Because we are good and because He is good so we shall be united

Our Deep And Lasting Respect For Heroes

Our deep and lasting respect goes out to all who lost their lives in war fighting for freedom and this includes journalists too and first responders.

In the battle for truth against the oppressor who lies we have already lost over twenty two war correspondents. How many thousands of medics, first responders, doctors, nurses and soldiers must die to feed the bloodthirst of Vladimir Putin and his oligarch allies? We know he has allies even in the Western Countries, politicians he endorses in France and the United States who embrace cheaper gas than ideals of democracy.

These Draculan allies of Putin Sacerdote must be exposed for what they are, whores and charlatans for the Buck: money rules them not ethics. There are over six million homeless refugees from Ukraine crowding into neighboring Europe which embraces and welcomes them. Let good outlast wickedness and evil of Putin and his cronies.

Those that want to divide Nato or withdraw from the Western ideals of democracy are traitors who must be led to the gallows and the

High Tower of London. There should be made a spectacle of them who worry more about their portfolios than their fellow man.

We are a band of brothers who join arms and forces to defeat the godless Bolsheviks who threaten our democracies and storm our Capitol buildings with ropes and fire axes.

The New Confederacy
OF Donald Trump

Many of us consider Russia to be the biggest menace but so is the new Confederacy of Donald Trump. It's no secret who Donald Trump's followers are: the Proud Boys and the great great grandchildren of Robert E Lee and sympathizers.

It may be true that many southern white families lost land and power when the slaves were freed. And the followers of Donald Trump are hoping that the Old South Shall Rise Again.

Everyone knows that the Kennedy's and Massachusetts encompass the far left which wants to bring socialism to America. This can be brought about best by taking away our guns. The Republicans have already done that disarming mostly Democrats and other Liberal Commie Rats.

It will be a glorious New America with Trump as King, the states abolished and replaced by Corporations. You employees will toe the line and work overtime to support the richest 3% or else!

Putin supports Donald Trump who likewise endorses Putin.

The New Order will lay down the law and the richest autocracies will attack and destroy every poor nation to colonize and exploit it or else.

So stay tuned to the mid term elections in the USA as the Republican Party is hoping to hijack both houses of Congress to overturn the last election and proclaim Trump our immaculate Fuhrer.

Vampires Steal Election

The vampires and vampire family are on the comeback with Vance winning Ohio with the endorsement of Trump. Ivanka plans to be the White House Press Secretary until her engagement to Putin is finalized. Putin's girlfriend will marry Trump. Trump backed by the Proud Boys and Klu Klux Klan will win the White House. The US will leave NATO and make a sweet alliance with Russia in order to drive down gas prices.

Meanwhile many women are protesting Roe vs Wade being overturned because the rumor has leaked out of the Supreme Court. Women's Suffrage will be repealed and only Christian soldiers will be qualified to vote in our New Roman Empire, Hail Caesar Donald!

Kushner will be sent to Israel as permanent Ambassador. Kamala Harris will be sent back to Sri Lanka and the majority of non white Americans will flee to Brazil.

The State Assemblies will be disbanded as the states themselves will be replaced by Corporations. KEEP YOUR JOB even if it means working at McDonalds forever. The Corporations will own almost all the real estate tax free for them of course.

Trump's sons will control the White House and patrol the grounds with lions and tigers.

America as you and I know it will cease to exist

Finland Not Living In Denial Prepares For Russian Aggression

Finland is not living in denial and has put its army in training for possible confrontation with Russia. Although there has been peace for almost eighty years the Finns who have had previous wars with Russia are preparing for the worst scenario with its worst neighbor.

Both Sweden and Finland are considering joining NATO, neighboring Denmark already has. Not too many of us remember the Winter War of 1938 when Russia attacked and eventually occupied Finland's capital. Finland evidently does and the Finns love sport and exercise. There is no better way to deter war than solid preparation. The United States has been at war from 9/11,2001 until a year ago but the short vacation is over now. Martin Lockheed is manufacturing Howitzers plus everything else.

Joe Biden's approval rating has been falling while Donald Trump who will back Russia and import Russian oil has been climbing with the white male population which evidently endorses him and his plan to leave Nato in order to ally with Kim Jongjung.

The US Supreme Court will consider repealing Women's Suffrage in order to eliminate support for Hillary Clinton who is a likely candidate as very much pro NATO.

Biden plans on a visit to the old age home to reminisce about all the wonderful years he can't quite remember as he has had a hard life and Dr. Jill will be assisting him daily from now on.

Stay tuned for a possible American Revolution to follow another Russian Revolution not to be confused with the soccer team Revolution. Women should take up arms. They most likely already have.

China which has stayed out of this big mess so far is warring with Covid resurgence in Shanghai, population over twenty nine million.

Iran will be purchasing Russian missile technology and satellite assistance in order not to be left out entirely in ongoing WWIII.

Makes Excuses For Invasion Blaming The West and NATO

Putin says that NATO won't listen to Russia or him: that elements of Nazism in Ukraine and West are planning for the demise of Russia who was the hero and ally who was instrumental in the defeat of Nazi Germany paying for it with a loss of twenty million people who are to be honored as having sacrificed them selves for the cause of the Motherland Mother Russia.

Not everyone who kills a Ukrainian babushka feels that she is a threat to the Motherland Moscow so this is more about Kiev's threat to replace Moscow as capital of the winner of this ongoing Russian Revolution which is information and democracy against this autocracy of Oligarchs like Putin who hold all the wealth and power, not all of whom endorse this Ukraine War wholeheartedly.

Putin who suffers some form of dementia and paranoia due to his psychosis from having killed so many people already is sharing his psychosis with the entire Russian population who is ordered to believe every one of his warped views on everything including his new very young sweet looking new girlfriend.

Fighting the Nazis somehow evolved in Russia becoming like the Nazis in order to triumph over Nazism Russia has created the New Man who is to believe everything Tsar Putin Sacerdote says.

Hitler once said that everybody enjoys a parade and certainly Moscow enjoys its Victory Day Parade the likes of which Trump wanted to employ in Washington D.C. until it was calculated in cost to the American taxpayers as being ridiculously extravagant and wasteful in resources as tanks would be tearing up the asphalt.

So Russia continues on its path of aggression against Ukraine, Georgia, Syria and anyone who would dare challenge her as she is now a full blown psychopath suffering from dementia and ignorance, her own lies to perpetuate another Dark Ages which certainly must be Putin's very dark mind lost in darkness.

It is the duty of every Western Country to hold a torch of illumination against this very Dark Plague of Putin who seems to be the Chief Rat.

Let us all be reminded why we have a Congress and elected representatives whom we trust that combined they can represent qualified mental health and restrain us from partaking in madness like that of Putin.

Sacerdote Putin Bloodsucker

Vladimir Putin, you are no longer held in esteem

There are many sons now missing on Mother's Day

Their blood ran deep into the Ukrainian soil

While fifteen million people are now homeless

And hundreds of millions may no longer have bread

So admit that you have become the Devil Incarnate

Everyone who cherishes his life is terrified

So now your enemies multiply while you steal more Ukrainian grain

The world goes into deep recession which indicates

High unemployment which can only be solved by drafting soldiers

There will be at least five hundred million of them

One hundred million of them will soon be on their way to Moscow

You will need over ten million missiles to protect yourself

You will need five million tanks and thirty million soldiers

I suppose you have solved the world's overpopulation problem

At least forty million Russians will die to add to ten million Ukrainians

Another hundred million people in NATO while COVID will equal or surpass battle casualties

Will all this blood quench your thirst as you must have lost your appetite for money

Everyone has been forewarned about the great reduction of humanity

Needed to combat climate change while this war will leave our planet unrecognizable

You too will suffer the same fate as we are all mortal

As for the memory of you it will be a four letter word now five

In Defense Of Russia

In the defense of Russia our former ally in WWII

Hers was a scientific experiment in international socialism

Because a weak Czar manipulated by Rasputin and other sorcerers

Disconnected the leadership of Russia from its people most of whom were serfs

Now the world is more literate and every teenager has an I-phone

You Russia can rejoin the League of Nations and be held in esteem

But you must disengage in this your imperialistic war of annexation

As for Putin himself psychiatric care is possible in even the worst of prisons

Understandably he is unfit to even stand trial of course it will be a Kangaroo Court

When you are complicit in killing four million people it is multiple capital punishment yes

Russia herself and her dissidents especially cannot be held accountable for your personal genocide

What else is there to say except I cannot defend your actions personally

I am just hoping the world will eventually forgive your people and nation

It will be spring again and green grass will sprout as well as trees bud

The dead shall not rise immediately but maybe when Jesus comes with the clouds

To make them all Angels once again everyone who has suffered because of you

Every social climber loves a fascist

Every social climber loves a fascist

After all they are well dressed and narcissistic

On his or her way up the corporate ladder

He comes from a good family with good credit

They all drive new luxury cars and even wash and polish them

Their families compile huge trust funds and dole them out to the faithful

Their very faithful worship money not God and are Republicans who profess Christianity

Without actually practicing charity or compassion but looking good in public is top priority

Or waving Old Glory at the Republican Convention

Democrats are dirty socialists covered in the mire of thieving

Because the poor are also unemployed since they don't tow the line

So once again all the countries will clash and the rich will defeat the poor

Please re-examine yourself to see where you stand and what has become of your life

If not a millionaire by now you are a leftist scum

This scenario is where we are headed as a nation no longer under God but money instead!

(Do you love Donald Trump?)

Poems To Putin

I must have received instructions in my sleep

That I should stop worrying about all those Ukrainians

Because I am an old man at least older than Putin

Older and wiser too at least I know to love because love conquers all not fear

So I am to retire now from all these poems and listen to thunder and see lightning

The Earth will correct all these imperfections of ours it will wipe out humankind

We will all go back to the Garden which is another universe entirely

Our suffering here will help us let go like Buddha did

There are uncontrollable events here on Earth like World Wars floods famines earthquakes tornadoes

So I wish peace for everyone and rest, a good night's sleep

The Nutcracker Suite by Tscachovsky will entertain small children and grandparents next Christmas Season

The land of Russia will somehow recover from its scars and wounds of having lost so many children likewise Ukraine

Trees and flowers will bud and young foals shall gallop to the delight of mare mothers

I too will grow tired of all this material chaos and indigestion I overate and overindulged

I will fall asleep and never awaken until I see Cherubs and Angels hanging the Stars

What will it matter then all my frustrations on this Earth all my lamentations

If I get sent to hell surely then I will meet Putin himself all we will roast there and eat too many spare ribs but never be full

I suppose now all my verses were inspired by television because I no longer read newspapers much

It was CNN War Coverage that inspired many of us to raise money and/or donate to UKrainian people, cats and dogs there as well

Dear Vlad, don't take this personally but when I see you I think of exploding atomic bombs so really I would rather not see you goodbye

I don't want you in my life nor in my poems adieu chao farewell adios
TH EEND

Telluride (a metal compound) called love by some

Windy whose hair is wild and free.

"Oh how you are unreliable but my love is undeniable

Who can tell that you're desirable

Will they see you're most admirable

Other girls giggle and tease

To win your attention will you please

Ignore their passes not stare at their asses

This is all such a farcuss don't rush off with them to have your heart broken

That will break both of ours, mine may not repair

From so many tares and far too many tears can't you see

You will love only me that I am the one

To fly you to the sun where we will melt and be one

I have to get dressed and go to work and I'm late

Spending too many hours and minutes dreaming of our date

You took me to the Drive-In and said you just can't wait

I said, "Not so fast, slow down it will be better in the long run take it slow"

When the movie ended you said you had to go

Is she still in the picture, the one who broke your heart

Who used you to win back her ex-lover she just uses you can't you see

You belong with only me and we'll fly off to Peru

Or paddle in Maine in your canoe I will go anywhere just call me

I'm waiting by the phone you promised you would

Are you talking to her instead she is just running you around

All over her town being her clown you'll never catch her she's too fast

She's her daddy's girl it will not last

She'll run home to her boudoir stare in her mirror perk her lips in the parlor

She's not for you can't you see I'm up here on the mountaintops

High on Mount Wilson there is a cold glacier a reserve of cool water to save you

From her destruction she is narcissistic and loves only herself she'll never love you

More she loves having stolen you from me can't you see her nasty plan

Her misadventure to win back her man while destroying us in her process

To rule the world with her evil laughter you think it's funny but Sonny

She's out to kill us and destroy our lives and true love

She doesn't need you affection she has her father for that which drives her mother crazy

All the money they spend on her to spoil her in her spectacle like a movie star

When she gets out of her car at the theater to step on a red carpet of your blood

Your heart will have melted and broken there will be nothing left of you

Your boss her lover will fire you and you'll be on skid row among broken bottles of champagne

Plus everything else God knows what she puts in your drinks

To lead you by the tie to make home movies under her ceiling mirror

No one else will ever want you because you gave yourself to pornogtaphy and voyeurism

Under the commands of her drunken lewdness she eschewed you with her lies

Now you will find yourself in a free fall into hell

I won't be there to pick up the pieces and your heroin habit

I'll be far away in my car speeding away from your Las Vegas nightmare you gambled our love

You threw the dice and lost you are so unreliable it's true and it's quite undeniable

That I fell for you and am still in love with my foot on the accelerator

I will have raced away off to Snowbird, Utah or Alta nearby for peace and tranquility

I met you in Telluride where we were like some precious metal compound

But you went atomic and broke away into your own element it seems and we are compounded no more

So I must set my sail on this tranquil lake and wait for some wind which shall I behold on the shimmering distant waves

I must sail on to find another more golden with which to wrap myself around and squeeze together in hot embrace

You were like fresh powder on a cold morning on the ski slopes but it was spring

The sun grew hot and you melted and there I was waiting for you by the ski lift in the slush

You must have turned left where I went right to follow her dangerous scarf in that breeze

Off you skied with both of them and to the bar where he talked business and became distracted so she feasterd her eyes on you and you fell for it the sucker you are

She led you off by your drunken tie and stole your cufflinks

I am in my Thunderbird leaving Snowbird and heading south toward the La Sal Mountains

I will lie half naked in that Moab sun after my offroad bike ride I will need a hot tan

All the more because you failed to be my man you're just a boy at heart too bad

It takes a man to win a woman's heart he has to wait for her by the door not run off

I will read about you at the breakfast table over my coffee I will sip to read your column

You were lost somewhere and no one can find you

So you are a "Missing Person" well I could have told them that ten years ago

You made a wrong turn and a poor decision and now you are somewhere near to "Where Love Can't Find You"

Maybe that's just down the road from "Hell" probably in Nevada as well

There is no water there and no snow I still have your skis you left in the ski rack

You won't be needing them I will have to sell them at the "Ski Swap"

So many pairs of used skis there it makes me wonder are there that many losers like you

It is a terrible world out there but I am back up on the mountain skiing under the ski lift

The powder is very deep and someone will notice me and I will smile gently and look away and pretend not to notice

And hope it's not you there's no second chance at love.

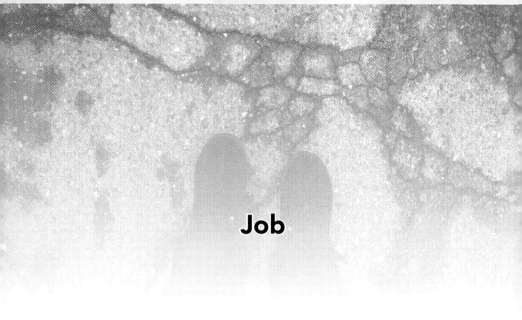

Job

My dear fellow Ukrainian you are like Job who lost everything

Who lost his entire family, his house business land and livelihood

Everything was taken from him because it belonged to God who gave
it all back

The Ukraine might be taken from you yes but you are to forgive them
and forget

They know not what they do nor did they know when they crucified

Our Lord

All of these crosses in the fields where lie your sons and daughters

Your grandparents and grandchildren they have gone to God to be

His Angels

Whereas Putin goes to the Grim Reaper and his fellow war criminals
straight to Hades

When there is nothing left to live for here on Earth you will live in

Life Everlasting

Our missions here on this Earth are very brief when compared to

Eternity

"My Sacred Heart weeps for you Ukraine but know you are My

Children"

Go now where you must and do your duty be My Servants go in Peace

Go in war if you must be a soldier then be one because life here is
mortal

Whether you be rich or poor a baker or a mortician a babushka or
a journalist

Remember to honor the Truth that "I gave My Life that you may not
perish but be raised likewise to Our Father"

Who is in Heaven let us have our daily bread but we do not live by
bread alone

But for everything that comes from God because it must indeed be

God's plan

The nations will rise and fall but God shall be there in the midst of
that sea of destruction

He shall walk upon the water and not drown and neither shall we

Ukraine

We are from Heaven and back to her we return in Faith and Love

Justice and Truth will be with us and we shall be free and noble

Because we choose the light and truth not darkness like Putin and his Oligarchs

Hell has been unleashed and that serpeant from Hades has found his lare the Kremlin

So we have chosen to resist deceit and lies and uphold the Truth and

Liberty

So help us God! Amen

Printed in the United States
by Baker & Taylor Publisher Services